Ripley's Believe It or Not!

Developed and produced by Ripley Publishing Ltd

This edition published and distributed by:
Mason Crest Publishers Inc.
370 Reed Road, Broomall, Pennsylvania 19008
(866) MCP-BOOK (toll free)
www.masoncrest.com

Ripley's Believe It or Not!
Taking Life to Extremes
ISBN 978-1-4222-1540-1
Library of Congress Cataloging-in-Publication data is available

Ripley's Believe It or Not!—Complete 16 Title Series
ISBN 978-1-4222-1529-6

PUBLISHER'S NOTE
While every effort has been made to verify the accuracy of the entries in this book,
the Publishers cannot be held responsible for any errors contained in the work.
They would be glad to receive any information from readers.

WARNING
Some of the stunts and activities in this book are undertaken by experts and should not
be attempted by anyone without adequate training and supervision.

Printed in the United States of America

Ripley's Believe It or Not!

TAKING LIFE TO EXTREMES

RIPLEY

PUBLISHING

a Jim Pattison Company

Taking Life To Extremes

Eccentrics of the world unite—discover the

marvelous mouth that can hold 210 drinking

straws, the remarkable lungpower that can blow

up a hot-water bottle, and be thunderstruck by

Miss Electra who survived two million volts of

electricity being passed through her body.

*Electrifying the audience, Miss Electra
sits on top of a giant tesla coil...*

Spiral Island

The English carpenter had thought about building his own island for a long time, and finally took the plunge just south of Cancun in Mexico.

RICHIE SOWA has created his very own tropical island paradise—out of 250,000 plastic water bottles.

The former carpenter from Middlesbrough, England, spent four years constructing

Paper Boat

In March 2003, comedian Tim FitzHigham rowed a paper kayak 160 mi (257 km) down the River Thames to break a 383-year-old record. In 1620, eccentric English poet John Taylor had sailed a paper boat just 40 mi (64 km) down the Thames before his vessel sank. Over eight days Tim rowed from Oxfordshire to London in a boat that was 85 percent paper, the rest being glue to keep out the water. When it did leak, he sealed the holes with sticky tape.

Spiral Island, a raft measuring 66 ft (20 m) by 54 ft (16 m) and floating in a lagoon off the exclusive Mexican resort of Puerto Aventuras. He began with a basic raft made from thick bamboo poles, stuffing the bottles, which he obtained from passers-by, into nets tied to the bottom of the poles. The air in the bottles helps to keep the island afloat and he has since planted mangroves, the roots of which grow around the bottles to prevent the man-made island from drifting. The real-life Robinson Crusoe has also nailed layers of plywood on to the poles to provide a solid base for his impressive house, which boasts two bedrooms, a kitchen, and a large living area with walls of plaited palm trees. The roof is covered with plastic sheeting, which collects rainwater for drinking. The mangroves that have been planted help to keep the island cool, and some of them now rise to 15 ft (5 m) high.

Richie Sowa relaxes on the desert island beach that he created just south of Cancun, Mexico, using 250,000 plastic water bottles that were donated by passers-by.

Richie's island home has a large living area, a kitchen, and two bedrooms. The walls are made of plaited palm trees and the roof of plastic sheeting, which also acts as a gutter to collect rainwater for drinking.

Food for Thought

Many prestigious art galleries, including the Museum of Modern Art in New York and the Tate Gallery in London, have purchased works of art made by a group of artists called Mondongo. Their pieces are unusual because of the choice of materials used in making them—cheese, cookies, plasticine, cooked meats, and chopsticks are just a few examples!

Tie Breaker

The world's longest tie—2,300 ft (700 m) long and 82 ft (25 m) wide—has been tied around the Pula Arena, in Croatia. When seagull droppings threatened to ruin the tie, the world's largest owl—a 7-ft (2-m) model—was brought in to guard it.

Chain Reaction

Making a paperclip chain is a serious business for California University student Dan Meyer. Not content with joining half a dozen paperclips, Dan linked 40,000 in one day in February 2004 to form a chain over 1 mi (1.6 km) long!

Coffee Break

The Stella Awards were inspired by Stella Liebeck who, in 1992, spilled a cup of McDonald's coffee onto her lap, burning herself. A New Mexico jury subsequently awarded her $2.9 million in damages. Her name is now used as a label for such U.S. lawsuits.

Ringing the Changes

Cinematographer Ed Lachman, who shot the hit movie *Erin Brockovich*, recently tried a new style of filming: Using Motorola V710 camera phones. He completed five two-minute videos by using six camera phones set at different angles. He projected the six images together, inspired by the works of cubist artists.

How the Cookie Crumbles

This portrait is made from cookies on wood by the Mondongo group of artists and was exhibited at the Daniel Maman Fine Art Gallery in Buenos Aires in 2004.

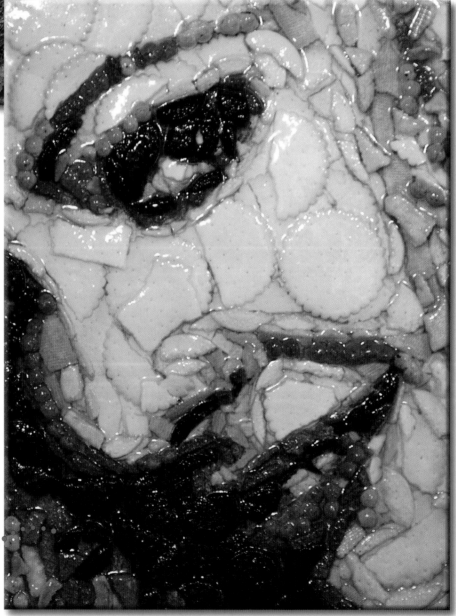

The Living Dead

Cary Sharp is known as Honorary Ghost 1,000 in Disneyland's Haunted Mansion after winning Disney's charity auction on eBay in 2004. For his $37,400, the doctor from Baton Rouge, Louisiana, got a personalized tombstone, complete with a humorous epitaph based on his interests and hobbies. Sharp even got to attend his own burial ceremony.

The Veri Thing

The Food and Drug Administration has approved a device called the VeriChip, an implantable computer chip to carry medical files. The size of a grain of rice, it uses radio frequencies to display a patient's blood type and other medical information when activated by a scanner in a doctor's office.

A Cold Snap

Audrey Twitchell of Colorado made her own skiing outfit from 600 Colorado State sales tax tokens, with a combined value of $1.20.

Tiny Guitar

A guitar carved out of crystalline silicon and no bigger than a single cell was made at Cornell University, New York, in 1997. Called the "nanoguitar," it is 10 micrometers long and has six strings, which are inaudible to the human ear. The guitar is so tiny that its shape can only be seen under a microscope.

Playing Away

Joe Cahn, of New Orleans, just hates to miss a single game. Therefore, each fall, for the past nine years, he has hit the road, crisscrossing the United States to attend both NFL and college football games at more than 50 different stadiums. Cahn estimates that by now he must have racked up nearly 300,000 mi (480,000 km) to appease his habit—and in all those miles, he hasn't received a single traffic ticket. The road is never lonely, he says, as he always travels with Sophie, his pet cat.

The Last Straw

Marco Hort in a recent record-breaking attempt managed to fit 210 drinking straws in his mouth!

The Big Picture
Two people were needed to turn one page of this gigantic 16-page book made by the Mazda car company in 2004. It measured 10 ft (3 m) by 11 ft 3 in (3.5 m), and weighed 776 lbs (352 kg).

Eco-logical
A Montana couple have built an environmentally friendly house for less than $15,000. Their cozy abode incorporates 13,000 empty soda and beer cans, and 250 used car tires in its foundation. The savings don't stop there: By heating the house with a wood-burning stove and solar power, the couple's utility bills are only $20 per month.

An Almighty Squash
In 2004, pumpkin-grower Joel Holland produced the winning pumpkin in the 31st annual Safeway World Championship Pumpkin Weigh-off, crushing the chances of 80 other pumpkins to win the prize. Holland had to use a flatbed truck to get his 1,229-lb (557-kg) pumpkin to the competition. To reward his green thumb, Holland received $5 per pound, making his total winnings $6,145.

Can You Believe It?
This replica of the Colosseum in Rome was made using more than 10 million used aluminum cans.

U.S.A.
Montana

It is illegal for married women to go fishing alone on Sundays, and illegal for unmarried women to go fishing alone at all.

No ORdiNaRY TootHpick!

IT'S AMAZING what Michael Drummond of Cocoa, Florida, can do with a toothpick and a magnifying glass!

More than 30 of Michael's toothpick carvings can be found in various Ripley's museums, including a cowboy complete with horse and lasso, and a butterfly alighting on a flower.

Even a cowboy with a lasso is no match for this miniature carving genius!

Butterflies on flowers are just one of Michael's carving specialities.

Take Your Pick

Bob Shamey of Ligonier, Pennsylvania, creates some of the world's smallest works of art. On an ordinary toothpick, he has carved ornate caricatures of golfers, sailors, fishermen, and aliens. He has even carved a nine-car freight train, and turned a toothpick into a miniature pair of pliers.

THE WORLD'S LARGEST JACK O'...

Jack O' All Lanterns

In 1982, the "king" of giant pumpkins, Howard Dill of Nova Scotia, Canada, grew the world's largest Jack-o-lantern. It weighed a mighty 445 lb (202 kg) prior to the carving, and measured 10½ ft (3 m) in circumference.

Catch Your Breath

Shane Shafer, 50, suffered seven months of constant, bark-like hiccups every four seconds before doctors implanted an electronic device in his chest in an innovative operation. All involved breathed long, hiccup-free sighs of relief when Shafer stopped hiccuping.

Watery Grave

A Florida firm offers an unusual resting place for cremated remains: A concrete case on the ocean floor. These "permanent living legacies" are linked to form an artificial commemorative reef in the waters off Palm Beach. Relatives who dive can pay their respects.

Floating Voter

James Pengov, 36, now knows that trying to sell his vote on eBay is illegal. In just 12 hours, authorities heard about—and shut down—Pengov's eBay listing. Pengov, who says he was just trying to pay some medical bills, didn't see the harm in voting for the party favored by his highest bidder, as he was unsure who to vote for.

Take Note

Cops picked up a Pennsylvania resident for passing counterfeit money: a $200 bill featuring George W. Bush. Clerks at the clothing store didn't know that there is no $200 bill. Nor did they notice that it was signed by Ronald Reagan, and that the back showed the White House lawn with signs saying "We Like Broccoli" and "U.S.A. Deserves A Tax Cut."

Steak a Claim

Barcley Prime, an upscale restaurant in Philadelphia, may offer the world's most expensive Philly cheesesteak. Its take on the city favorite, which includes Kobe beef, goose liver, sautéed *foie gras*, caramelized onions, and shaved truffles, costs $100. By comparison, typical cheesesteaks, which are usually made with thinly sliced ribeye steak and American cheese, run at around $4.

Banana Republic

More than 6 tons of bananas from the Canary Islands were used in the world's first banana pyramid in Madrid, Spain.

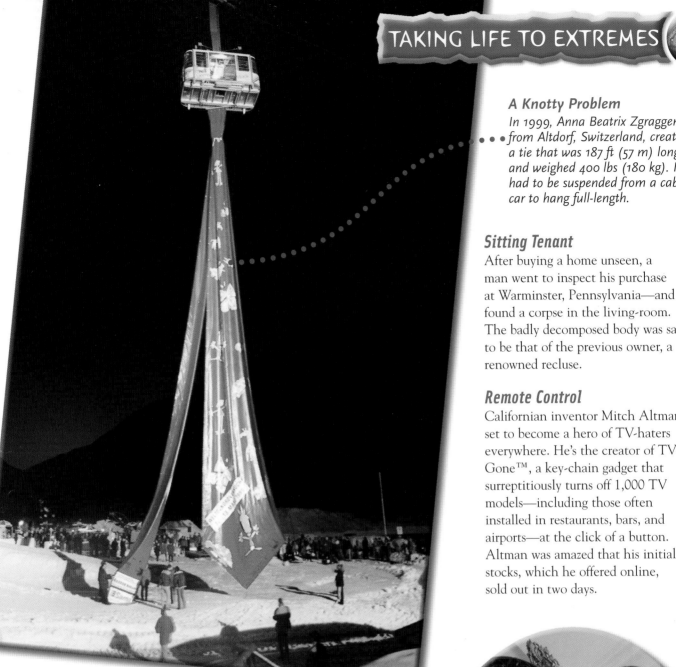

A Knotty Problem
In 1999, Anna Beatrix Zgraggen, from Altdorf, Switzerland, created a tie that was 187 ft (57 m) long, and weighed 400 lbs (180 kg). It had to be suspended from a cable car to hang full-length.

Sitting Tenant
After buying a home unseen, a man went to inspect his purchase at Warminster, Pennsylvania—and found a corpse in the living-room. The badly decomposed body was said to be that of the previous owner, a renowned recluse.

Remote Control
Californian inventor Mitch Altman is set to become a hero of TV-haters everywhere. He's the creator of TV-B-Gone™, a key-chain gadget that surreptitiously turns off 1,000 TV models—including those often installed in restaurants, bars, and airports—at the click of a button. Altman was amazed that his initial stocks, which he offered online, sold out in two days.

Fire Starter
A Washington teenager is in such a hot seat that he'll be lucky ever to sit down again; at least in his off-road vehicle. While joyriding—without a condenser—the 18-year-old sparked a forest fire that burned 16,000 acre (6,475 ha). The U.S. Forest Service planned to bill the teenager $10 million to help pay for the costs of fighting the fire, as it is required by law to do so.

Right on Cue
In January 2003, Jack Nemeth, Doug Prenevost, Harlan Ivarson, and Doug Webster played pool continuously for 103 hours in Brooks, Alberta.

Ashes to Ashes
A San Francisco company thinks cremated remains should be displayed in style—and it offers some unique holders. One is an urn made from a liquor cabinet that plays "How Dry I Am" when opened.

Lock, Stock, and Barrel
Vadim Mikhailyachev, a teacher from Russia, and his students made a giant lock that weighed 880 lbs (400 kg). The key weighed 35 lbs (16 kg).

Going Bust

Canadian professional gambler Brian Zembic accepted a $100,000 bet in 1996 that he wouldn't wear female breast implants for a whole year. Not only did he wear the implants and win the bet, but he liked his new 38C breasts so much that he was still showing them off four years later. Brian is no stranger to crazy bets. He previously won a $30,000 wager by spending an entire month in a bathroom.

TOP FIVE
WEIRDEST MUSEUMS

1 **Frog Museum**
Münchenstein, Switzerland

2 **National Museum of Pasta Foods**
Rome, Italy

3 **European Asparagus Museum**
Schrobenhausen, Germany

4 **British Lawnmower Museum**
Southport, England

5 **Bowling Ball Art Museum**
Safety Harbor, Florida

Baby Boom

Michelle Duggar, 37, of Fayetteville, Arkansas, gave birth to her 15th child in May 2004. With the exception of two sets of twins, her children were born one at a time— and all their names begin with "J."

Fast Text

In 2004, British cell phone engineer James Trusler laid claim to being the world's fastest texter. He typed a message requiring 160 taps in just 67 seconds live on Australian TV.

Empire Building

The "smallest model of the world's tallest building," this model of the Empire State Building (when it was the world's tallest building), created by Curtis Mathews of Tennessee, took four years to complete. It measured 19½ ft (6 m) high.

14

The Smallest Largest

THIS TRAVELING MUSEUM is one of a kind!

The World's Largest Collection of the World's Smallest Versions of the World's Largest Things is a display of miniature replicas of oversized sculptures found across the U.S.A. by founder and curator Erika Nelson. She photographs the many giant objects she passes, and collects information about the sculptures. Then she makes and displays a miniature replica along with the information in her museum!

The World's Smallest Version of the World's Largest Canadian Goose is seen here photographed with its namesake in Sumner, Missouri.

The World's Largest Collection of the World's Smallest Versions of the World's Largest Things museum is situated in none other than a converted Ford Econoline bus!

Domino Effect

A Chinese woman, Ma Lihua, sent the world domino-toppling record crashing in 2003. She took seven weeks to line up 303,628 dominoes (stretching for 9⅓ mi or 14 km) and they came tumbling down in just four minutes. The only threat to her record attempt had come from a stray cockroach, which, during the painstaking preparation, had knocked over 10,000 tiles.

Ma Lihua poses for photos with her toppled dominoes after completing her record-breaking feat.

Festive Farewell

Ozella McHargue adored Christmas, so when the native of St. John, Indiana, died in 2004, her family gave her a Christmas-themed funeral. Even though Ozella died in September, her family decorated the funeral parlor with holly, mistletoe, and a Christmas tree, and instead of somber, funereal music, mourners listened to festive classics such as "Rudolph the Red-Nosed Reindeer."

Love and Death

A Canadian couple were married in a funeral chapel in 2001. Shane Neufeld and Christy McKillop chose the unconventional venue in Winnipeg, Manitoba, not only because he worked there, but also because it was where they met.

Body Snatchers

Two desperate thieves stole a hearse from outside a Philadelphia church just as it was waiting to take a corpse to a cemetery. Fortunately the corpse wasn't in the vehicle at the time.

Hide and Go Seek

Author Michael Stadther gives treasure-seekers a challenge in his new book, *A Treasure's Trove*. In it are clues to where he's hidden 12 tokens that can be redeemed for real jewels. It took eight years to find good hiding places in public areas across the United States.

Blowing Hot and Cold

Known as "the fire-proof man," Singlee was a performer at the Ripley Odditorium in Chicago in the 1930s. He is shown here putting a blow torch to his bare skin, including his eyes.

U.S.A.
New Hampshire

You may not tap your feet, nod your head, or in any way keep time to the music in a tavern, restaurant, or cafe.

Jump Ship

Stuntman Robbie Knievel, son of Evel Knievel, jumped seven military aircraft on the deck of an aircraft-carrier in a stunt to promote the launch of a movie about his daredevil father.

Dead Heat

Spiritualist Emma Crawford was buried in 1890 on Red Mountain, near Manitou Springs in Colorado. A landslide in the 1920s suddenly sent her coffin hurtling down into Manitou. Each Halloween the event is commemorated in the Emma Crawford Coffin Races, in which competitors dash along the streets of Manitou carrying coffins containing live Emma look-alikes.

Dead Man Talking

Mourners at a chapel of rest in Belgium were horrified when a mobile phone rang inside a coffin. The undertaker had forgotten to take it out of the deceased's clothing.

Shark Meat

British property developer Robert Blackwood wants to be fed to Great White sharks when he dies. His bizarre request was inspired by a TV documentary on the sharks.

Rainbow Warriors

About 31,000 Filipino students from the Polytechnic University of the Philippines gathered in Manila to form the world's largest human rainbow in 2004.

It's Electrifying!

Dr. Dean Ortner used to perform brain surgery on mosquitoes in his former role as a research scientist. Now he's left his lab coat behind to go on the stage, but he still demonstrates his love of science in his "Wonders of Science" programs. His trademark is "riding the lightning," in which he passes a million volts of higher frequency electricity through his body. The power generated makes a board burst into flames, and sends bolts of blue lightning shooting from the fingers of his other hand. He has performed this feat once a week for 30 years, yet he says he's suffered little more than a few burns on his fingertips. The higher frequency doesn't interfere with his nervous system, yet there is still enough power to ignite the wood.

Million Volt Man
Flickers of ionized krypton, xenon, argon, and neon lightning dance around inside a globe, attracted to the touch of Dean Ortner, the Million Volt Man.

Ice and a Slice?

With a room temperature of −5°C (23°F), the Absolut Icebar in Milan, Italy, has to be one of the coolest places to spend an evening!

Pay Your Respects

A man from Schopfheim, Germany, was so keen to save on funeral costs that he tied his dead mother's coffin to his roof rack and drove her along the motorway to the cemetery.

Worm's Eye View

His body wrapped in saran wrap, Welsh performance artist Paul Hurley spent nine days slithering around a field in 2004 to see what life is like as an earthworm. He spent his time burrowing, pausing only to eat a leaf or grain of soil. He saw this as "an exploration of the earth and dirtiness." He has previously coated himself in jelly to become a slug, and dressed as a snail and licked the inside of a greenhouse for two hours.

Off-color

Georgia company Collegiate Memorials allows college football fans to go to their graves proudly displaying their loyalty. The company makes special caskets and urns emblazoned with a university's colors.

Smoke Signal

A Romanian smoker made a coffin out of more than 7,000 cigarette packs in 2001. Mihai Cepleuca said he wanted to be buried in it to show that smoking really can put people into their graves.

Turkish Delight

Thousands of Turks helped to carry the world's longest national flag through the center of Istanbul in 2003. At 2.4 mi (3.6 km) long, the flag was created to mark the 80th anniversary of the foundation of the Turkish Republic.

Lightning REacTioNs!

DANIELLE STAMP, otherwise known as Miss Electra, electrified the audience with her dazzling performance for the Ripley's TV show.

As she sat on a giant tesla coil, 2 million volts of electricity were passed through her and out of her fingertips. To top it all, she didn't feel any pain!

Lucky Strike

Being struck by a lightning bolt wasn't that bad at all, according to John Corson, even though the bolt went through his body and then tripped three circuit-breakers in his garage. Since it happened, the 56-year-old says he has been feeling positively energized—he even goes so far as to say he feels ten years younger.

The shocking performance illuminates the audience watching eagerly outside the Ripley's Odditorium in Hollywood, California.

The sparks can be seen flowing through the coil and up into the air, passing through Miss Electra.

Participants hold up two light strobes at which Miss Electra fires bolts from her fingertips!

The Farmer Wants a Wife

An Ohio man paid a farmer to carve the words, "Michelle, will you marry me?" into his corn crop. The bride-to-be melted into giggles—and said "Yes"—when she spied the message from a small plane.

All Hands on Deck

Christina Shaw exhibits a 16 ft (5 m) deckchair sculpture at the Three Counties Show held in Worcestershire, England.

Buried Alive

A 50-year-old Czech man, Zdenek Zahradka, claimed a new world record in June 2004 by surviving for ten days buried underground in a wooden coffin without food or water. He lost 19 lbs (9 kg) in weight during his ordeal and said he spent most of his incarceration sleeping.

Balanced Diet

Students from Brigham Young University in, Provo, Utah, balanced 1,290 hand-held eggs simultaneously in 2003. In the course of balancing the eggs, the students broke only half a dozen.

Round the Clock

Jay Larson, founder of the International Speed Golf Association, shot a 72 on a 6,500-yd (5,945-m) course near San Diego, California, in just 39 minutes 55 seconds, averaging less than two-and-a-half minutes per hole. Under the association's rules, the number of strokes is added to the time to calculate the player's score—in Larson's case, 111.55.

No Ordinary Joe

Mastocytosis is an incurable disease that affects approximately one person in every 500,000. Joe Tornatore is one such person: He experiences anaphylactic shock whenever a foreign substance, such as the venom from a bee sting, enters his body. While participating in a two-year immunotherapy program, Joe wore a beekeeper's suit to protect himself every single time he went outdoors.

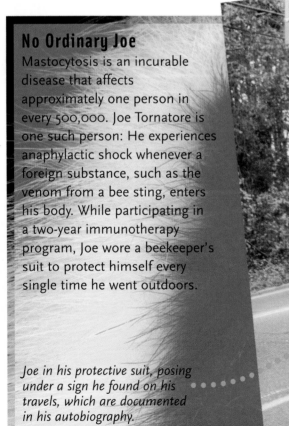

Joe in his protective suit, posing under a sign he found on his travels, which are documented in his autobiography.

Fast Acting

In 1995, Canadian Sean Shannon recited the 260 words of the "To be or not to be" soliloquy from William Shakespeare's *Hamlet* in just 23.8 sec.

CRAZY GOLF

- American golfer Maud McInnes took 166 strokes on a par-three hole in 1912 after she tried to play the ball out of a river

- Rick Sorensen completed 18 holes at Meadowbrook Golf Club, Minneapolis, in 86 strokes—blindfolded!

- Canada's Moe Norman once teed off in the Los Angeles Open with a Coca-Cola bottle

- In 1914, British golfer J.N. Farrar accepted a bet that he could complete a round in under 100 while carrying full military gear, including rifle and rucksack. He shot a 94

- Australian golfer Rufus Stewart played 18 holes in total darkness in 1931 without losing a ball. He went round in 77

In the Swim

Environmental activist Christopher Swain, of Portland, Oregon, jumps right in if needed. His latest feat was swimming the 80 mi (130 km) of the Charles River, in Massachusetts, to ensure the Environmental Protection Agency keeps to its goal of making it swimmable by 2005. Parts of the river are badly polluted with sewage, trash, and pesticides.

Big Cheese

A South African hypermarket made a 122 ft 8 in (37.4 m) pizza, using 9,920 lbs (4,500 kg) of flour, 1,984 lbs (900 kg) of tomato puree, 1,984 lbs (900 kg) of tomatoes, 3,968 lbs (1,800 kg) of cheese, and 1,763 lbs (800 kg) of mushrooms. It took 39 hours to prepare and cook.

Holy Smoke!

It took New Yorker, Vincent Pennisi, seven years to create this 38-in (97-cm) high wooden model of Milan's cathedral.

Cookie Monster

A giant chocolate-chip cookie, baked by the Immaculate Baking Company in 2003, weighed in at a staggering 40,000 lbs (18,150 kg). Displayed at Flat Rock, North Carolina, it took eight hours to bake, and required 30,000 eggs and a cookie sheet the size of a basketball court!

Have Your Cake and Eat It

In 2004, Serbian baker Zvonko Mihajlovic unveiled what he claimed was the world's biggest birthday cake. Thousands of residents of Nis tucked into the 400-ft (122-m) long cake, which weighed more than two tons and used 2,100 eggs and 1,500 lbs (680 kg) of sugar.

Bouncing Back

In 1999, David Kirke, of the Dangerous Sports Club, celebrated the 21st anniversary of the first ever bungee jump by repeating the leap off the Clifton Suspension Bridge in Bristol, England.

HiGh FlYiNg!

AS IF WALKING along a beam from one hot-air balloon to another at 4,000 ft (1,220 m) wasn't daring enough, pilot Mike Howard complicated his feat by wearing a blindfold!

The two balloons had been tied together in the skies over Bristol, England, to prevent them from drifting apart. It took Mike a nerve-wracking three minutes to walk the 19-ft (6-m) beam. He then parachuted to the ground to meet his wife and daughter.

Cruise Control
Stuntman David Fish drove a car at 3,500 ft (1,067 m)—strapped to a balloon by steel cables. This wasn't his first hot-air feat. He'd previously had a pillow fight at • • • • • 5,500 ft (1,676 m), on a bed suspended from a balloon.

Chilling Out
Ian Ashpole relaxed in the comfort of a hammock strung between two hot air balloons, before freefalling and parachuting to the ground.

Armchair Traveler
Balloon pilot Pete Dalby floated above Bristol, England, in the comfort of his own armchair, which had been strapped to a specially adapted hot-air balloon.

Madhatters' Tea Party
In 2001, stuntmen Julian Saunders, Rob Oliver, and Ross Taylor became the first people to take tea atop a hot-air balloon. After having tea at 4,920 ft (1,500 m) over Melbourne, Australia, they rapelled down the side of the balloon back into the basket.

Raise a Toast

A half-eaten grilled cheese sandwich sold on eBay for a whopping $22,000 (£15,000). Diana Duyser put the toastie up for sale on the Internet auction site because she was staggered by the likeness of the Virgin Mary that the sandwich bore. The page was viewed more than 100,000 times before the auction ended.

Diana Duyser said she was shocked and scared by the likeness at first, but then put the sandwich up for auction to share the miracle with others.

Pushing the Envelope

When Jeff Datwyler picked up a stray envelope off an Ohio street in 2004, he assumed it was trash. When he opened it, he found a check for $15,000. The irony is that, across town, the person who had lost the envelope was standing in a bank line, blissfully unaware that he'd lost his deposit. Just as he was reaching into his pocket for the envelope, his bank notified him that it had been found.

Short Circuit

The World's Shortest St. Patrick's Day parade took place on March 17, 2004, in the town of Hot Springs, Arkansas. The town staged its parade on Bridge Street, the thoroughfare which, at a quarter the length of a normal city block, has a claim to being the shortest street in the world.

Brought to Book

New York student Steve Stanzak spent seven months sleeping in his university's library because he could not afford accommodation costs. He was finally discovered in April 2004.

A Rise in Inflation

Manoj Chopra of India inflated a hot-water bottle at the World Strongman Cup to display the extraordinary power of his lungs.

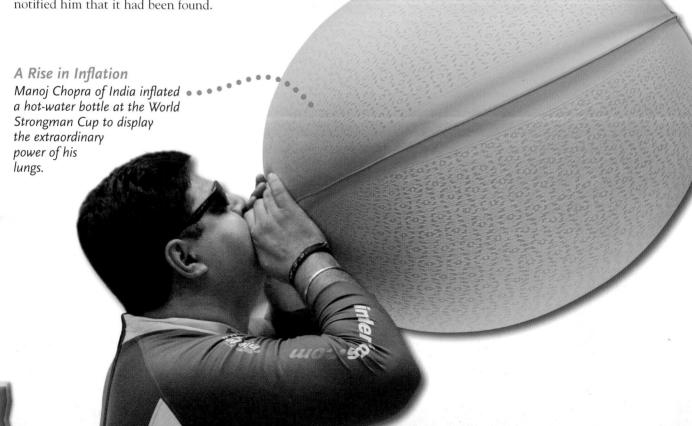

BANANA GEORGE

George is known to everyone as "Banana George" because of his love of all things yellow. He wears yellow clothes, drives a yellow car, and bounces across the lake behind a yellow speedboat.

GEORGE BLAIR learned to snowboard at 75, drove a racing car for the first time at 81, made his first parachute jump at 82, and took bull-riding lessons at 85!

Age has never been a barrier for the extreme sports fanatic who is now in his nineties—he made just as much of a splash in 2004, when he was pulled along Florida's Lake Florence at 40 mph (65 km/h), as when he went waterskiing barefoot in icy Antarctica when he was a youthful 71. George's favorite fruit is the banana, and most of his possessions are yellow, even his sunglasses and phone—hence his nickname, "Banana George." In 2002,

Sports Illustrated for Women put George in the magazine's annual swimsuit issue. "I had never thought of myself as one of the world's sexiest men," he admitted. "But I like it."

George is the world's oldest barefoot waterskier.

He publicizes his favorite fruit so well that he gets sent free bananas.

A Tight Squeeze

In 2003, 14 people from the Kabosh theater group from Belfast, Northern Ireland, squeezed into a phone booth in Edinburgh, Scotland, to break the world record by two people. One said: "It was pretty claustrophobic, but it's a quick way to get to know people!"

U.S.A.
Nebraska

In Waterloo, barbers are forbidden from eating onions between 7 a.m. and 7 p.m.

Tip of the Iceberg

Entitled "The Ice Cube Project," this red iceberg floating in Ilulissat Fjord in Greenland, was created in two hours by artist Marco Evaristti, using 792 gals (3,000 l) of paint, seawater, three fire hoses, two ice-breakers, and a crew of 20 men.

Layer Cake

In 1953, Primo Maca of California baked this 15½ ft (5 m) tall giant cake, which fed a total of 10,500 people!

Pillow Talk

No fewer than 645 people took part in a mass pillow fight in the town square at Gannet, Kansas, in June 2003.

Heavy Reading

Michael Hawley, a scientist at the Massachusetts Institute of Technology, has written the world's largest published book—a 133-lb (60-kg) tome entitled *Bhutan: A Virtual Odyssey Across the Kingdom.* Measuring 5 ft (1.5 m) by 7 ft (2.1 m), it used 1 gal (4.5 l) of ink and enough paper to cover a football field. The author admitted: "It's not a book to curl up with at bedtime—unless you plan to sleep on it!"

Pole Star

A former pilot with the Royal Canadian Air Force, Jack Mackenzie joined a nine-member ski expedition to the North Pole in 1999—at the age of 77! To reach the Pole, the sprightly septuagenarian had to ski for up to seven hours a day.

Be Dazzled!

At $22,700 (£15,250), Dazzle is surely the world's most expensive cocktail! A concoction of rosé champagne, strawberry liquor, lychee liquor, lemon juice, and syrup, topped with a white gold and diamond ring, it certainly dazzled diners at the Bar & Brasserie of Harvey Nichols department store in Manchester, England.

The cocktail was part of a "Pink Dinners" month, during which the menu featured an abundance of pink items, from raspberries to pink champagne.

Flower Power

Melvin A. Hemker of St. Charles, Michigan, grew a sunflower in 2001 that had 837 heads and was so heavy that it needed three wooden braces for support. The previous record for a sunflower was a mere 129 heads.

The Pony Express

Indian policeman Sailendra Nath Roy pulled a bus by his ponytail for 100 ft (30 m) in 2003. Previously, he had pulled a van and a jeep with his ponytail and lifted a 45 lb (20 kg) weight with his moustache.

Watt a Bargain

A 40-watt bulb in Fort Worth, Texas, has been burning non-stop for nearly a century! The bulb, which cost just a few cents, was originally fitted above the backstage door at the Palace Theater on September 21, 1908, with orders that it was never to be switched off. Still going strong, it now lights up the Stockyards Museum.

Global Village

In 2001, 13,588 "Village People" danced to the song "YMCA" before a baseball game in Omaha, Nebraska.

Small Talk

Dwarf-tossing contests, such as this one in Surrey, England, are exactly what they sound like. Some say they are offensive, but when the State of Florida banned the pursuit, 3 ft 2 in (96.5 cm) performer Dave Flood sought to overturn the decision so that he could continue to earn a living.

Reaching His Peak

Salvation Mountain near Niland, California, is America's craziest peak. Made from hay bales and adobe, topped with a giant cross, it is 100 ft (30 m) wide and rises three stories high above the desert. Leonard Knight, a former car mechanic who built the mountain 17 years ago, has defied government attempts to demolish it, and lives at its foot in an old truck without electricity or water.

Gift of the Gab

To celebrate the start of her 19th season on U.S. television, talkshow host Oprah Winfrey gave every one of her 276-strong studio audience a brand new $25,000 car.

Man Bites Dog

A 23-year-old man from Bend, Oregon, suspected of assaulting his girlfriend, bit a police dog on the head as he tried to avoid arrest. The dog, named Amor, had just bitten the suspect on the leg.

Baby Bell

Steve Hough is the proud owner of the world's smallest working bell-tower, which he built in his back garden in Gosport, England. Named "Little Ben" it's a tribute to its larger namesake, London's Big Ben.

Pushing His Luck

A man was arrested in Blue Lake, California, in 2004 after police officers saw him doing one- handed push-ups in the middle of the State Highway 299. He was trying to get a lift home and thought his daring fitness routine would force a driver to stop for him!

Wind Bag

Solicitor's clerk Paul Hunn from London, England, trains on an unusual diet of carbonated drinks and spicy foods. Why? He is the world's loudest burper! In 2000, Paul belched at 118.1 decibels—as loud as a pneumatic drill.

Butter Nuts

A Swedish couple out hunting in the northern province of Jaemtland were alarmed to stumble across 70 pairs of shoes, all filled with butter. Sneakers, stilettos, and boots were all stuffed with 1 lb (0.5 kg) of butter and-spread out over the landscape.

Binocular Vision

Frank Gehry designed this spectacular binocular-shaped building in Venice, Los Angeles.

SupEr SculpTurEs!

THE U.S.A. IS HOME to a spectacular range of oversized sculptures.

Minnesota is littered with such attractions, and one of them is a 33-ft (10-m) tall statue of the legendary lumberjack Paul Bunyan, in front of the Paul Bunyan Historical Society Museum in Akeley.

High Point, North Carolina, the self-proclaimed "Home Furnishing Capital of the World," boasts a 33-ft (10-m) chest of drawers. The attraction has stood there since the Chamber of Commerce built it in 1926.

The 12-ft (4-m) prairie dog statue in Interior, South Dakota, stands guard outside The Ranch Store souvenir stand. Not only can you see the world's largest prairie dog statue here, but you can also feed or even buy real prairie dogs.

Hair Pin

Who would have thought that it's possible to drill holes through a human hair? J.M. Thompson of Philadelphia did—each hole, shown below, measured 0.0007 in (0.002 cm)! Howard Adam of Wisconsin even managed to thread a human hair through a drilled hair.

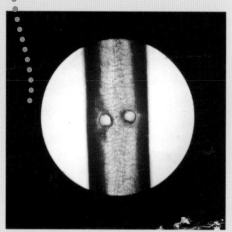

Riding High

Life is one long rollercoaster ride for Chicago university lecturer Richard Rodriguez. He has been setting rollercoaster endurance records since the 1970s, and in 2003 at an amusement park in Berlin, Germany, he set a new mark of 195 hours. He used two trains for the attempt, one car on each being equipped with a small toilet, as well as cushions for him to sleep on.

The Sound of Silence

In February 2003, musicians in Halberstadt, Germany, played the first three notes of what will be by far the world's longest concert. They have stretched a 20-minute piano piece by avant-garde American composer John Cage to last… 639 years. The concert actually started in September 2001, but as Cage's piece began with a rest, there were 18 months of silence leading into the opening notes.

Toilet Humor

Unusual flying machines were the theme for the 2003 coastal flying demonstrations in France. Approximately 8,000 pilots gathered to exhibit their wacky flyers, such as this slipper-happy paraglider.

Licence to Thrill

Fred Hale Sr. of New York got his driving licence in 1995—at age 104. He carried on driving until it expired on his 108th birthday.

The Smallest Show on Earth

Spending £1,000 ($1,500) installing soundproofing, a projection booth, and velvet seats from his local Odeon theater, Englishman David Alligan has converted his garden shed into a cinema with an 8-ft (2.5-m) screen.

Cool Customer

In January 2003, Jin Songhao broke his own record by standing naked in freezing conditions for four hours. The 48-year-old stood in a quiet spot near Harbin, China, in temperatures that plunged to –29°C (–20°F).

Melting Point

A 2004 attempt to break the world record for the longest hockey game was abandoned after a full 87 hours and 10 minutes of play because the ice in Edmonton, Alberta, began to melt—due to unseasonably high temperatures. The players were trying to break the existing record of 130 hours and 7 minutes set by the Moosomin, Saskatchewan, Moose Fraternity in 2003.

Get the Message?

Mexican Laura Carmona made her message loud and clear to boyfriend Alfonso Hernandez when she covered his car in love letters on St. Valentine's Day!

Taking the Plunge

A Canadian prankster plunged into the pool during the men's diving competition at the 2004 Athens Olympics wearing a tutu and tights!

Dead Ringers

The funeral of Dane Squires was interrupted in 2004 when the deceased phoned his family to say he wasn't dead! His sister had identified him as the victim of a railroad accident in Toronto, Ontario, but the burial was put on hold when Dane called to say that the mutilated body was someone else's.

Leap of Faith

Fitted with artificial knees and a hearing-aid, 92-year-old Herb Tanner completed his first parachute jump in 1998 when he leaped from a plane 3,500 ft (1,067 m) above Cleveland, Ohio. A pilot for 63 years, Herb had always wanted to make a parachute jump, but his wife had threatened to leave him if he ever did so. When she died in 1996, he was finally able to make his dream come true.

Stamp of Approval

The German Post Office in Berlin promoted their building by covering all 130,000 sq ft (12,000 sq m) of it with thousands of love letters.

InDex

ACKNOWLEDGMENTS

Jacket (b/l) South West News/Rex Features

6 Sam Barcroft/Rex Features; 8 (t/l, b/r) Marcos Brindicci/Reuters; 9 (b) Action Press/Rex Features; 10 (t) Masatoshi Okauchi/Rex Features, (b) Alessia Pierdomenico/Reuters; 12 (b) Desmond Boylan/Reuters; 13 (t) STR/Reuters, (b) Sipa Press/Rex Features; 15 Erika Nelson/World's Largest Things/www.WorldsLargestThings.com; 16 (t) David Loh/Reuters; 17 (t/r) Chip East/Reuters, (b) Romeo Ranoco/Reuters; 18 (b/l) "Red Boots Productions", Hollywood, CA, USA, (r) "Wonders of Science", Whittier, CA, USA; 19 (t) Andrea/Rex Features. (b) Stringer/Reuters; 22 (t) Matt Cardy/Rex Features; 23 (b) Adrian Sherratt/Rex Features; 24 (dp) Paul Gillis/Rex Features, (b) MMP/NAP/Rex Features; 25 (t) United Television News/Rex Features, (c) South West News/Rex Features, (b) HO/Reuters; 26 (b) Dan Riedlhuber/Reuters; 27 George A. Blair; 28 (sp) SCANPIX/Reuters; 29 (t) Howard Walker/Rex Features, (b) Picture Partnership/Rex Features; 30 (t/c, t/r) Phil Yeomans/Rex Features, (b) John Powell/Rex Features; 31 © Amy C. Elliot; 32 (b) Sipa Press/Rex Features; 33 (t) Andrew Winning/Reuters, (b) Action Press/Rex Features.

All other photos are from Ripley's Entertainment Inc.
Every attempt has been made to acknowledge correctly and contact copyright holders and we apologize
in advance for any unintentional errors or omissions, which will be corrected in future editions.